Rules Of The Game

I am giving you the ball, son, and naming you the quarterback for your team in the game of life. I am your coach, so I'll give it to you straight.

There is only one schedule to play. It lasts all your life, but consists of only one game. It is long with no time out and no substitutions. You play the whole game all your life.

You'll have a great backfield. You are calling all the signals, but the other three fellows in the backfield with you have great reputations. They are named Faith, Hope and Charity.

You will work behind a truly powerful line. End to end, it consists of Honesty, Loyalty, Devotion is Duty, Self Respect, Sturdy Cleanliness, Good Behavior, and Courage.

The Goal Posts are the Gates of Heaven.

God is the referee and sole official. He makes all the rules, and there is no appeal from them.

There are ten rules. You know them as the Ten Commandments and you play them strictly in accordance with your own religion. There is also an important ground rule. It is, "As ye would that men should to you, do ye also to them likewise."

Here is the ball. It is your immortal soul! Hold on to it. Now, son, get in there and let's see what you can do with it.

Faith On The Field

The Pastoral Ministry of a Coach

Tony Johnson & Anthony Di Giovanni

About The Authors

Tony Johnson

Currently the Athletic Director of W.T. White high school in Dallas, Texas. Tony has 27 years of experience in education, coaching and creating a culture that reflects his desire to make a difference in athletics and education.

From coaching at powerhouse schools like TCU, A&M and even leading as the Head Coach at two NAIA programs, Tony has worked with and coached for some of football's elite. Tony is a published author who enjoys public speaking. Tony currently resides with his family in Dallas, Texas.

Anthony Di Giovanni (Johnson)

Anthony is High School Football Coach & Teacher, as well as an Independent Filmmaker, Videographer, and Author. Anthony's other books are *Everyday A Scene*, *The Millennial Vision*, and *The World Soul*, all available on Amazon.

Acknowledgements

This book is dedicated to my father, Fred Lee Johnson, and all the coaches along the way who impacted me. My dad was my first coach. It's been said that if you can't discipline in your own home, then you can't really help others. My father was not perfect but did show me the love of God.

My father once told me, "Do you want me to coach to be great? Or Coach you the way you want?" It was his way of saying this "game" or life as we know is full of ups and downs, and along the way you need guidance and mentors to inspire you. You play to win, but sometimes you lose. Losing is a part of life, but if we remember Christ's love for us we truly never really lose. So thank you, Dad. Thank you for loving sports and for connecting us through them.

I would also like to mention my wife and children. Mary, my wife, is my best friend and my rock! She has supported every move a coach can make. She is honest with me and never lets me feel too low or get too down on myself.

To my kids, you are all so wonderfully gifted. You all have a 1st Corinthians 12 mindset. You are all unique yet talented and you are all guided by your faith.

Never lose that. I love you more than you will ever know. There are four of you, just like four quarters in a game, where there are quarters you need to put them all together to win in the end. Your closeness as siblings is one of my greatest victories. Never lose your love and respect for each other. Thank you for allowing me to coach you for life! Love, Dad.

Table of Contents

Pre Game:
Your Life Is The Gridiron

First Quarter

Second Quarter:
Cultivating Your Ministry As A Coach

Third Quarter:
Not Everybody's Big Time

Fourth Quarter:
The Train Stop

Overtime:
Collection of Essays, to bring home the Victory

Pre Game

Your Life Is The Gridiron

By Anthony Di Giovanni (Johnson)

My dad was a coach and still is, so it goes without saying that I've grown up in the sport my whole life. My earliest memories are of me and my brother playing around the football field as my dad was coaching practice. The sport was never something I had to learn to love or commit to and for a while I could never tell anyone why that was. For the longest time I couldn't pinpoint the "WHY", the reason I stuck to it all the way through college. But now that I've graduated college and am out of the game, I've been able to turn around and objectively view the game, and the experiences I've had in it.

I'm not a jock by any means, and I'll tell anyone who tries to label me as such that they really don't know me. I have a Bachelor's degree in Film, co-own two production companies, love drawing, love writing my own screenplays and then turning them into films and also love writing books. So I never viewed myself as a jock. I'm also a full time coach and teacher now in high school so although not fully a jock, I still have that athletics prone side to me. But like a jock may say, Football is an amazing sport, that I think everyone should play it. To me, Football is a mirror image of life. As I've gotten older and entered the "real world" I see things, occurrences, circumstances, situations happening that are metaphoric to things

I've already gone through and conquered while having played division one college football. But it's not just at that level that these circumstances or situations are navigated, it happens on all tiers of the game. What I'm referring to are things like suffering. Do you realize how mutual suffering is so important to the alliance of strangers? When I look back on the hell we freshman went through our first summer together at the University of North Texas, I realize we had to be put through those gut wrenching moments that wanted to make you quit, so we would turn to our teammate next to us, or the roommate we had. We were forged in fire together and it made us closer, as a class and as a team. This happens everywhere at every school, but it also happens in real life. You and the guy next to you are both up at 5 am for freshman practice, it's your first year coaching and you have such big goals and dreams, but none of them involve messing around with freshman practice at 5 in the morning. BUT it's this tough time that is bringing you closer to the staff around you whether you know it or not. Suffering is necessary for growth in comradery. There are many other ways we face suffering in our daily lives, and that's just because we're human, living in a sin filled world. But I can promise you, have no doubt, I'm better equipped to face any type of suffering because of what I've gone through physically and mentally in football. I have more confidence in victory in my life, because of the small victories I made continually throughout my experiences in football.

In going through the ups and downs of walking on at a division one school and then eventually earning a scholarship, I learned a lot. And the importance of mutual suffering is just one of them. I'll touch on some more later in the book. But it's here that the title of my preface needs to be explained further. "Your life is the gridiron," is not meant to be interpreted on a surface level. What I'm saying is that the gridiron, the field, the game, is all one mirror image of life if you choose to look at it like that, and learn the lessons it can teach you. Life is a game; life is the gridiron; the playing field. You have to look past the surface. I had no choice in being brought up in a life of football, but looking back, I'm so grateful that I was, and that my dad kept me in this lifestyle. Yes it's a game, but it's a game that teaches you so much. So it's more than a game. It transcends that definition, and becomes an educator on life.

My dad was my coach for most of my youth, and was my position coach all of high school. Though I'm not playing these days, he is still my coach in many ways. Whether it is in the form of him literally being my head coach as I help him out on Friday nights, or my life coach, he's still guiding and teaching me. One night while we were out smoking cigars on the back porch, he told me about this concept of America's history that involved a transitional phase in its timeline and somehow tied with coaching. I immediately knew it would make a great conversation I would want to have with many people around the world. I pushed my dad to the conclusion that writing it as a book would be the best way to accomplish this large conversation.

~Anthony Johnson

First Quarter

"What is past is prologue."
~ Shakespeare

Chapter 1
When I Knew I Was A Coach

Not everybody can be a coach. It seems like a glamorous job to the world and it can be rewarding. The great Bill Parcells once said that "Eventually the train stops for everyone." I don't know when that time will be for me. Maybe it has passed me by, maybe it hasn't. I'm currently in my 27th year of coaching and I still find many blessings within the role of "Coach", and I still find purpose in attempting to affect young men's lives. Lou Holtz in his book, "*Winning Everyday*" says "You have to have a sense of purpose. Understand what you are trying to do."

I remember the night that I knew what I was born to do. It was January 2nd, 1984, the Orange Bowl game between the Nebraska Cornhuskers; the most prolific scoring machine in college football, and the upstart Miami Hurricanes. The Hurricanes were flamboyant, outlandish, brash, and excitable. My father had always raised me that acting that way was not part of the game. Character counted for something, he said. So, I gravitated towards Tom Osborne. The greatest coach in all of college football in my mind. The man I tried to mold my career after, and fell short so many times. I've coached under and with many great men, men like Dennis Franchione, and have only met Coach Osborne a handful of times. Yet even never having coached with or played under the man, he has still impacted my coaching and faith. I am not perfect and will never be. I am, however, forgiven. I have made a choice largely because of men like coach Osborne to let Christ be a part of my coaching philosophy.

I watched those 1983 cornhuskers every Saturday because I lived in a big 8 country. I was born and raised in a suburb of Kansas City, Kansas. A town called Olathe. Rich in football history.

I watched those Huskers demolish and destroy every team they played, but noticed how they always did it with such grace and class. Tom was always the one to praise the other team at press conferences; yet when talking about his own team, always praised how disciplined they were. It was amazing, something to see. It didn't hurt that many fine men from my hometown, Olathe, Kansas, went on to play at this university. But that night, January 2nd, the Nebraska Cornhuskers went for a two point conversion to win it all. Back then you couldn't go into overtime, you either had to go for two or stay in a tie. The Cornhuskers wouldn't tie, even though it could guarantee them the national Championship and number 1 seed. The

Miami Hurricanes would have lost with a 31-31 tie, but Tom never wavered in his decision making process. He thought for a second, called his play and then waited for the outcome. I watched in wild amazement as Turner Gill rolled to his right, threw the pass, and the ball was tipped by a Miami Hurricane defender and went through the hands of the Nebraska running back. Game over. I was devastated and tears began to roll down my face. How could this man that my dad said had so much class and character lose? Doesn't the good guy always win? Doesn't the bad guy always lose? Doesn't good always triumph over bad? In my fourth grade mind, I was struggling to comprehend these circumstances and these events. I was trying to make sense of it.

In the game of football, sometimes you lose. That's part of the development of anyone in sports. But that night I learned so much. I watched Tom Osborne hold that press conference and I saw the pain in his eyes and the pain on his face. I was relating to him. I was connecting emotionally to his situation. So much so that my dad had to console me through the night, even having to tuck me into bed later.

The next morning, as I moped around, my father told me that there was something I wasn't getting about that loss. He told me that what Coach Osborne had done, the decision he had made, had earned him so much respect from the world of coaching and those outside of it as well. I never forgot that moment and never will. It was at this time in my life that the seed was planted in the back of my mind. The seed that would grow into the desire and passion for me to be a football coach.

Chapter 2

Today, we as a society have so much. I mean we have so much materialistically. There are any number of technological needs and wants to be made and met. I think anyone would admit, that as a whole, in our century, in our day and age; we are a bit pampered and spoiled in comparison to how things were for our grandparents and great grandparents. There's nothing inherently wrong with this truth though, or wrong with technology either. Everything comes back to the user. But today, the user can get anything they need, do anything they want (within law) and BE whomever they want. So the question must be asked: "Why be a football coach?" A good question. To grow on this question one could even ask: "Why coach at all?". Or: "What's the importance of a coach?" I will never forget one day when I was a little boy grocery shopping with my Dad. I was 7 or 8 years old and a young man came up to us and said "Hey Coach!" and I remember being so confused. Who was this kid talking to? Then my Dad proceeded to talk to this young man and I could see the adoration on the face of this young man. I was seeing my father in a different light. He was a mentor to this young man. I realized at this moment that my father was important in this young man's life because he was his Coach. Coupled with these questions about coaching, are questions we've asked ourselves, as well as heard others asking. Questions like: "Why are there so many fathers missing from the lives of children?" And "Are we living in a fatherless society?" It is my belief that these questions about coaching and fatherhood are related. There are two component parts that flow through our current society. My objective with this book is to answer these questions. To even begin to find answers to these questions we can't look around to our present time and our current societal structure. We must go back.

***

Go back with me, to a time when there was barely any technology, especially not technology like we know it. I'm talking about the pre industrial boom in America. It's time to go back to before the Gilded Age and actually a little before the Progressive Era as well.

Depending on who you talk to, these times we are looking at were right around the late 1800's and leading into the turn of the century. This was a time of great change in our American Story.

We find the family still growing up and living on acres of land with livestock and fields of various crops. Towns and cities are not nearly as prevalent and definitely not close in proximity. Going to school was sometimes rare for children. Generally, a farmer would raise his son and daughter to also become a farmer, naturally, as they spent all day everyday working with and helping dad. This was a hard working life for everyone involved. Most families were having to get up at the rising of the sun and immediately get to work. The chores of the day would have been feeding the livestock, cleaning out corrals, planting and harvesting crops. This was tough labor. On top of that, there would have been chores that were more maintenance; like repainting barns or rewiring fences. In an Agrarian society there wasn't a lot of luxury for anyone especially the youth. Agrarian means that the whole country was in a state of farming. The structure of society at this time was following the frontier and the expansion westward. Exploration of American land had come to a halt for the most part. At this time, in America's youth, it was time to cultivate the land. The family as a unit was extremely tight knit and children in this setting learned the cultural behavior they needed to survive in everyday life from their parents. You would possibly even see what would become a traditional school curriculum being taught by mom when there wasn't work to be done. Boys became MEN, by watching, and learning from the MAN of the house; Dad. But as we all know, time continued on and genius men & women created and tinkered and soon the American people saw their world rapidly changing around them. In a quick span we as an American society went from what was called "Agrarian" to "Industrialized". This created major changes in the family and at-home life. Primarily, for most families, it now meant dad didn't get up and work out back, he got up and LEFT for work in the city. For the first time, mass amounts of children were about to start being raised with Dad "gone at work", for most of the day if not all of their day. This also meant, dad's availability and time to teach these boys and girls how to be adults became increasingly narrowed. Where were they to turn to learn the cultural necessities? Most moms were able to still stay home and work the day to day chores, and this was great for daughters. Unfortunately though, as we've established, everyone had to pick up their own weight in helping the family unit run as a living body and the mother in this shifting of the society took on a lot of the responsibility to uphold the house.

There may not have been enough time to discipline the boys. I believe most would likely agree with the opinion that having a male presence around a youthful boy helps.

On top of this industrialized shift in the family life, going to school became more of a priority in the life of children. Education became more important to the family structure and it allowed children to be among peers and in turn clash and clang against each other as they worked out their cultural differences and awkwardness. With the organization of schools, came the organization of sports teams. Now there was another shift in the home life, especially for boys. This was a key shift, as this change now saw the COACH being put in the place of an authoritative male figure in most young boys' lives. Children are usually competitive by nature whether that's playing at who has the best toy, who is the fastest on the playground or all time king in four square. Sports attracted the competitive. Children usually have good intentions, but they need guidance. No team is made by one person and with this fact everyone must come together as a cohesive whole to make victories a possibility. But a child, a young adult, cannot lead other children in the ways necessary for this cohesiveness. To be that kind of leader you need patience, experience, and the ability to see the broader picture. We have all been young; we probably didn't have one if any of those things. This is where the adult coach came in to act as the essential piece, the guiding star. Most people acknowledge a coach is valuable for these reasons. BUT, it is less acknowledged that most coaches spend more time with these children than do their parents, depending on how involved with sports the child is. And that's something that hasn't changed over the years no matter what state we have been in as a society. It has definitely been a factor ever since the concept of "Dad went to work," was born.

So, knowing this fact, a fact that some parents don't like to admit, then one should start to put a significant amount of importance on who it is that is coaching their child. My son is a coach. My dad was a coach, and all of us wouldn't argue against it, that most parents don't put this importance on who is coaching their child. If you're a parent reading this and have never thought about the coaches of your child in this way, then hopefully that will change after this read.

Chapter 3

I want to call attention to the parallel of this scale of importance though. On one side of the scale there is the weight of importance that falls on the parent when deciding who it is their child plays for and is spending most their athletic time around. Across the way, on the other side of the scale is the importance of the COACH, to figure out who he or she is. It is the coach's responsibility to figure out and establish themselves, not only to the players they will be in charge of, but also to their peers, and the rest of the community. How will you be remembered? A sixteen year old running back once approached me after a game early in his career and said, "You were the only man to believe in me." That player said "man", not coach, and it threw me off at first. But it stuck out forever in my career. Jim Valvano said once, "My father gave me the greatest gift anyone could give another person, he believed in me."

Are you, as a coach, putting importance on who you are? If you are in agreement to the fact that in certain ways, the responsibility of being a shining example of manliness or womanliness falls on the coach, then you must admit that these coaches have to be intentional with their actions. They are shepherds leading a flock, not just towards winning games or how to block, but towards victories in life. Having all once been children, we cannot deny that for the most part kids are great at hiding their hurt, especially as they get older. So being a surface level coach, one who just shows up to practice and gets through the workout solely focused on the win they want at the end of the week, is wasting the kids time and their own time. You must, as a coach, become cultivators of men. I have always said I see coaches fall into many categories. Some we'll talk about coming up, but three important labels of a coach I've used are: "Called", "Covert" and "Clueless". "Called" and "Clueless" can be worked with and trusted. After all, you can teach a coach that's "clueless" to the reasons why he's here or what his purpose is. But if you're a "Covert" coach, you usually have double standards and are seeking only self gain, and you can't be trusted.

I must admit, in my youth of coaching, a primary goal was winning games and championships. However at the same time, I knew that high school football was the end of the line for most of my players. That's why I have always viewed football as a vehicle to prepare young men for a life of character. I believe that football will make you a better businessman, co-worker, husband, father or church leader.

You're shepherding these children into adulthood, and whether you know it or care to admit it, they are looking at you. These players are sub-consciously taking in your words and actions as equal to what a man is in our society. Are you being the right representation of the modern man? If you're skeptical about this thesis and this mindset, then how can you argue against the certain relationships the world has seen between player and coach? The relationships where a player became more than that word and the coach transcended that title.

Comparatively, coaches therefore are very similar to a different kind of shepherd in our lives; the Pastor. Just as a coach, in the church the Pastor is the leader of the body and is a public figure that many are turning to as an example. And just as a coach, the Pastor's relationship transcends title and position with certain relationships to church members. It is this parallel, the pastoral ministry of coaching, that we are going to dive into, interpret, and help make easier. In the parts to come, we're going to talk about how best to cultivate your ministry, how the definition of a man is formed in today's society and how that affects boys, and how you should be defining what the "Big Time" is in your life.

Cultivating Your Ministry As A Coach

"We have to separate WHO we are,
from WHAT we do."
~ Jim Tressel "Winner's Manual"

Chapter 3

If you're not a coach at the junior high, high school, college or pro level, you may never have taken a moment and truly thought about the concept of coaching and the extreme amount of risk it implies to job security. Essentially, a coach is putting their job, their income, their financial security, in the hands of children and young adults. Regardless of how much we argue against it, the fact of the matter is that coaches are ultimately judged at the end of the day by wins and losses. We coaches on the inside know that there is obviously more to be judged than just wins and losses. Tom Osborne said, "Success, as far as I'm concerned, cannot be measured in terms of wins. It's more than winning. It's how close we're coming to playing as well as we can. Becoming the young men that God has called us to be. By this measure it's possible for more people to feel better about themselves as athletes and coaches."

It's unfortunate at times, there are examples of amazing people being judged as inferior or fired because they haven't won enough games. Pepper

Rogers once said, "There are two types of coaches: those that have been fired and those that will."

I have been fired, it's not fun. You go through the gamut of emotions. You feel like a failure like you have let your kids, team, family, friends and self down. The game can get ugly. It can break your heart and it is tough to be a part of this ministry and that is exactly what it is, a Ministry. I am blessed with a loving wife who has moved all over this country and put up with multiple changes as I have chased college and high school jobs. Oftentimes the wife is left behind to pack up the house, withdraw the kids from one school and enroll them in the next. It takes a toll. I have always prided myself on taking care of us in all these moves, still I have seen how losing a job can affect your ministry or make you cold to wanting to trust again at the next job. As a family, I wanted us all to know I would take care of us and that all was going to be good if we just trusted God. A pastor also has to move a lot and plant churches etc. I imagine the congregation gets tired at times of the same voice just like a team sometimes will.

One must remember that if God brought you to it he can bring you through it. Every life and every season has broken dreams or cracks in the road. It is in these moments when we must realize that Christ is walking with us. And then allow him too! He is going to get the glory in your situation.

Pastor Steven Furtick says it this way, " you are not a hostage to your situation, you are a weapon." A weapon for God. I have tried to teach my son, and my family this through my trials in coaching.

In a book titled "The Message" it reads, "*He comes alongside us when we go through hard times, and before you know it, he brings us alongside someone else who is going through hard times so that we can be there for that person just as God was there for us. Your hard times are also our hard times.* 2 Corinthians 1:4-7"

Over the years, I've seen it myself, that there are coaches out there that leave the profession because of the pressure THEY put on THEMSELVES. That pressure can always come from external factors taking many forms and we'll talk about those soon, but a lot of times it's the pressure to win or to be the best that negatively affects a coach and hinders their outreach and influence towards the young men underneath their lead. There is a flip side to every coin and this case is no different as I know there are coaches out there that have so many victories, so many trophies, but internally they are self centered and blind chasing win after win. In both cases, we must put on a lens of Christ-like understanding and realize that as sinners and as humans in general: we fail. We lose in many different ways sometimes. We're not perfect and never will be, but one thing the gospel teaches us is that we are forgiven. Speaking on the two sides of a coin brings to mind Frosty Westering's great book, "Make The Big Time Where You Are" where he dedicates a whole chapter not to one side or the other of the coin, but to the edge. Frosty explains that it's the edge that sits between trying to be number one on one side of the coin, and doing your best on the other side. In this scenario, the edge represents giving it your all. We'll talk more about Frosty's book in a bit.

It is this way that we should look at the coaches we know that fit into both the previous mentioned categories, the two sides of the coin. A coach should be striving to also teach this outlook on life and loss to their players at all times. That's easier said than done, trust me I know.

***

It is also through this way of looking that we should look at ourselves, coaches, when we stare in the mirror. When we lose sleep at night worrying about if there was more we could've done this week or more we could have said. It is through this lens of forgiveness, (and in forgiveness received, God's certainty), that we should look when we're wondering if we're going to win enough games this year to not get fired.

It is through this lens of forgiveness and realization, that we as coaches aren't perfect, that we begin to turn inward. It is here that we begin to circumnavigate the foundations of who we are as a person and as a spirit filled vessel on this earth. This is a good start, but hopefully it leads you further and further inward until you've found change starting to happen externally. Hopefully, one of those inward journeys has you pondering on who you are at the current job you're at, but also in relation to your future.

What I mean to say is that you should ask yourself if you are a "Builder" or a "Stayer" ? A builder is one who in our definition, gets to a job and puts in as much as they can to build that team up towards victory on the field, in the classroom, and in life. They strive for incremental increase, and with enthusiasm forcefully grasp for change. They begin a fire, but "Builders" then move on to start another fire elsewhere as the flame they started at this school begins to burn bright for another and possibly many more to come. Builders leave for various reasons, and let's admit that sometimes it is in pursuit of promotion or ambitious gains. These things are not inherently bad or sinful; its how much they influence us, where that line can begin to be crossed. Speaking on "Builders" reminds me of a great poem called, "The Builder" by an unknown author. The poem reads:

I saw them tearing a building down

A team of men in my hometown.

With a heave and a ho and a yes yes yell,

they swung a beam and a sidewall fell.

And I said to the foreman, "Are these men skilled?"

"Like the ones you'd use if you had to build?"

And he laughed and said, "Oh no, indeed...

the most common labor is all I need...

for I can destroy in a day or two

what takes a builder ten years to do."

So I thought to myself as I went on my way...

Which one of these roles am I willing to play?

Am I one who is tearing down as I carelessly make
my way around?

Or am I one who builds with care, in order to make
the world a

little better... because I was there?

~ Author Unknown

On the flipside of the Builder is the "Stayer". A Stayer usually receives an assistant position of various levels. They invest and they work their tail off. They put their chin down and just climb and claw and remain. That is one thing they are for certain: Stayers are constant. They are consistent. And then they look up and in time they have now been moved into a position to take over as head coach. And they'll get it and they'll stay there for years and years slowly kindling their own fire of change in their team. At times, a stayer can be possibly mistaken as passive or slothful to the outside as they stick around through the worst of it and always make it. But they aren't these stereotypes, they are just wired a different way than other types of coaches. And that is perfectly fine.

We aren't trying to typecast coaches and pin them down to only two categories. Undeniably there are many different types of people and personalities in this world. Yet in general, I have been in many different programs and have seen that a lot of coaches come down to these two types or forms. Again, neither is wrong as some men are cut a certain way that they just fit one lifestyle better than the other. Why we're calling these things to attention is because you as a coach must take the time to think about which of these are you? It all goes back to being able to sit down and figure out who you are as a man, which leads to you being able to know who you are as a coach and then in doing so, know who you will be to your players. In consequence, this will effect what identity your team will take. Some reading this may have thought they knew which category they fit into. But it never hurts to take some time and review. Reevaluate who you are, where you have been, the major decisions you've made and the impact they have had on your life. What hardened and forged you into the coach you are now? Why do you believe in these certain core values? Why is it important for a child or young adult to know these things? We as humans sometimes go through life and get so caught up in it that we lose sight of who we are and whose we are. So never be afraid to take the time to slow down, and reestablish your identity.

Here are some practical steps to figuring out if you're a "Builder" or a "Stayer" if you're still trying to answer that:

1. Ask yourself where you want to be in 2 years? 5 years? Is it the same school?

2. Are you ok with putting in the work to get things going in the right direction where you're at now, and not seeing that come to its fullest fruition in a few years from now?

3. Dwell on the truth that there is a consequence to every action. If you're realizing you're a builder, and wanting to move around every year or two, realize that this will have effects on your resume, and how people view you in the future if you ever decide you do want to try and invest in something a little more long term.

Chapter 4

These questions and scenarios we've presented, are all to funnel you inward initially. Inward investigation is the threshold to external change. The external change we seek as coaches is to become the most efficient and influential leader is it not? We were all once those competitive kids and in many ways still are. Hopefully that competitive vigor filters into your pursuit of becoming the best you, and in turn becoming the best coach.

Once we've begun the inward journey we will begin to see change in our cultivation of the flock that is our team. But one thing we must always be aware of is the wolves in the wild that wish to harm our herd. These wolves are all the external forces pulling on you as the coach in many different forms. The wolves of outside forces come in many shapes and sizes such as drama prone parents, employees who misunderstand your motives, bosses with unrealistic expectations and more. If we are not too careful, and give more attention to a wolf here and a wolf there, then the herd will come under attack from the rest of the wild pack you never saw coming and the sheep will scatter. How we avoid this downfall is by keeping vigilant watch. We must constantly be aware of the wolves out there, BUT we must not let them consume us, our time, our thoughts and care. Let it go and let God. Be prayerful about it all, and then turn your attention to the matters at hand.

***

A pastor has to deal with the same concepts. As a shepherd of the church, they are constantly surrounded by the various wolves of life. A good pastor will turn to his ultimate coach, the coach with the most wins in the universe, God, when feeling the pressure of the wolves closing in on his herd.

While on the subject of pastors and their similarity to coaches, we interviewed a pastor from the Village Church Denton, based out of Denton, Texas named Brad Welkker. Brad is a young pastor in his mid thirties who at the age of 23, started coaching baseball and worked at Seminole State College in Oklahoma, University of Arkansas, Little Rock, and ended his career at Dallas Baptist University before entering the life of ministry. When asked how coaching helped develop and prepare him for pastoral ministry, he said that one of the most important things he learned as a coach was people themselves. He learned how to listen to the different types of people and their personalities. As a coach he had to assist all these different people with their own personal goals, and with the group towards accomplishing a bigger team goal. He was able to lead young men down a path towards victory. As a pastor, Brad says that nothing has changed in that regard as he's still trying to lead a bunch of people with their own personalities, lifestyles and goals towards one ultimate goal which is being more like Jesus everyday. As a coach Brad had to learn to be adaptable when it came to his educational verbiage and technique with different players as not everyone learns the same. The objective was always the same with each player, but sometimes they would need to have the practice of that objective molded towards their learning style. Again Brad says that nothing has changed in pastoral ministry with the consistent objective being serving Christ and molding our hearts to be more after His.

Adding to this advice of putting importance on studying people and putting them in a position of leadership, Brad also went on to say that naturally as a coach, you form relationships with kids on the field. It was in these relationships that he was always trying to hammer home consistency. Brad needed his players to consistently work hard at practice, and then in turn consistently perform on game days. It didn't help the team or the overall goal if as a player, you were great one game, and then helpless the next seven games. But he emphasized that this consistency transcended gameplay and filtered into consistent lifestyle off the field. Brad was always challenging his players to be consistent in school work and studies, as well as their morals. Ultimately, if he couldn't trust them to handle themselves properly off the field when he wasn't around, then he couldn't trust them on the field. I think in some form or fashion we've given similar talks to our players we've coached. But like Brad we must as coaches not just say these things, but take the initiative to be present. We as the coach must be the initiator, the catalyst of change in these children's lifestyles and morals. Like Brad we must take the time to get to know each one, no matter the size of the team, so then in turn we can take the time to learn how they learn. Then, on top of this action, you must be consistent with it. You can't as a coach demand consistency, and then yourself not be consistent. That goes with punishment, celebration, attitude and energy. They must all be consistent as a leader. That type of leading by example, while also demanding the same from those around you, will get the flock to follow the shepherd. There's a great saying that sums all this up; "Kids don't care what you know, till they know that you care." Go show them you care.

While I worked at TCU in the beginning of my career, I was yelling at a player for not catching the ball in a drill one practice. Over and over I yelled, "Catch the ball!" The player's demeanor changed as he slowly became defeated. Chris Thurmond, an assistant with a heart of gold leaned over and told me, "Hey, he's not trying to drop it. Coach him up!" I realized then that I needed to put more intention and thought into the fact that words carry power. Especially when those words fall on youthful ears.

You've read from a pastor himself that coaching and pastoral ministry are two realms that look awfully similar. So why is it so hard to take some time and imagine the pastoral influence you have over your team. Why can't you right now start looking at your influence as a coach, and see it as just as important and just as infiltrating as that of a pastor's. Why can you not decide right now to not only be the technical guide showing the ins and outs of the game, but also be the spiritual, Christ like example for your players? When you take the time to shift your gaze inward you don't only find out more about yourself, but in there, if you look correctly, you'll find God. Call to him, and grow close to him as you learn more about who you are. As you take these steps towards God and his ways, you'll begin to become a shining example of his works in the world around you and to the world of the children you're coaching.

A couple ways that I attempt to show kids I care about them:

1. Be INTENTIONAL with them: Have meaningful conversation, not just surface level questions about their day. That's how the convo gets started, but find time to take it deeper. The best way to do this is to keep asking questions; keep digging.

2. It may be uncomfortable at first, but tell kids you love them. If you're one of those people that has to mean what you say, search for the love you have for a kid just as a human being, as a soul driven creation of God. Then you can say it and mean it, and eventually begin to get to know them enough to mean it for different reasons.

3. Greet every kid at the door on their way to the locker room or practice. When the bell rings, I rush to the entrance of the field house, and fist bumps every kid with energy and excitement.

4. During practice, during down times, become a student of body language. Body language is going to help you feel the pulse of the team. Start studying the kids around you.

5. Dr. Billy Graham once said "A coach will impact more people in one year than the average person will in an entire lifetime"

6. Introduce kids to FCA (Fellowship of Christian Athletes)

7. Be a change agent for good

Some studies done out there say 97% of all people in the world are influenced in some manner by sports. In our sports-first driven world as we know it today, athletes and coaches have a greater influence than most parents and teachers. They are the role models, good or bad, whether they realize it or not.

Third Quarter

Not Everybody's Big Time

"If the game of life ended tonight, would you be a winner?"
~ Jim Tressel "Winner's Manual"

Chapter 5

We've talked a lot about our society so far. Our American cultural history a bit, as well as our behavioral societal views and morals. Amazingly all of it tying into being a coach and more specifically, a Football coach. One issue in today's world and theology that we haven't addressed is ego. It's an issue everywhere and that's because humans are everywhere. If you think about it, we just naturally start everyday thinking about "I". It's a battle to be selfless in our actions and in our thoughts and that's just how we're wired. It'd be a naive thought to believe that this fight doesn't filter into the Christian lifestyle. In fact as a Christian, I've had a lot of talks with non-christians and just non-believers in general, and they almost always criticize and stereotype Christians as self centered and judgmental. Now this may be because of ONE person they met that treated them so in the moment but still, it's a criticism we should nonetheless be aware of. I think we should especially be aware of this criticism as faith based and spiritual coaches because as a coach, you are automatically a faith based and spiritual LEADER. With that said, we'd like to recall the cruci-fixion as described in the gospel of Luke. Speci-fically, Luke 23:39-43. It's here that we get the only account of the thief on the cross next to Jesus. It's this story that I think is one of the core pillars of Christianity. Why? Well what's the thief say? He recognizes Jesus and recognizes that Jesus doesn't deserve what's being done to him. But he does admit to Jesus that as a thief, he DOES deserve what's being done to him. Then the thief ends it with humbly asking Jesus to just remember him when he gets to heaven. Jesus replies that he'll do much more than just remember him (Luke 23:39-43). At some of its most essential teachings, Christianity says to all of us, we are all thieves, and deserve to be crucified. Jesus was not a thief, he was perfect, and took on our punishment for us. We are to look at Jesus and say exactly what the thief did, "Lord, I am a thief (Sinner) and you are not. I deserve punishment, but you do not. Yet you still took it for me, and my sin." The bible also mentions how all our righteous acts are like filthy rags (Isaiah 64:6). Therefore, there is literally nothing we can DO to get to heaven. Jesus is the only salvation. This concept is a really hard thing for us as Christians and just humans in general to grasp. You're telling me, God, there's nothing I can do? Nope. Accept Jesus into your heart and take it. Think about this; most of us, even when someone surprisingly gives us something, for the most part we are thankful but immediately have a desire to reconcile this good deed and begin thinking of ways to pay it back. At least that's how I am. But God is like no, there's literally nothing you can do. Take my GRACE and MERCY. We're all thieves being granted a gift we don't deserve. So how could we not approach leadership, coaching, and just life in general with courageous attempts at humility?

One of the ways that I like to remind myself to be humble as a leader, as a shepherd to my flock, is to remind myself constantly, "Not everybody's big time." This saying has a couple layers and I love it so let me dissect it a little. This school of thought originated from the aforementioned book, "Make The Big Time Where You Are," by Frosty Westering. I found this book at a pivotal time in my life and it helped mold my outlook. It's a wonderful book and you should go find it right now if you haven't read it.

As I have stated earlier I am from Kansas and grew up watching and admiring coaches like my high school coach Gene Wier, and my first Division one boss in Dennis Franchione.

Coach Franchione gave me my first job, one that I will forever be grateful for. I used to tell my son that coach Fran, as he is affectionately known, was one of the most organized driven men I had ever met. Coach Fran was so driven that he (as stated in the newspaper after his firing from Texas A&M) never took time to smell the roses. It was always about the next big job. If you get to truly know Fran you see that he was fighting against religion growing up. A man that lost his mother young and had a father commit suicide, coach had questions about his faith and a chip on his shoulder. Later in life, with his own cancer scare he would begin to realize how much of a positive impact that God actually had on his life.

Coach Fran climbed the ladder of success quickly and is a great example of who I wanted to be. More importantly coach Fran, and subsequently me, realized that your coaching tree and championships are not the goal. The goal is making the big time where you are!

Initially, this statement, "Not everybody's big time," refers to the person vocalizing it. In my youth, I was chasing. Much like Coach Fran and my other coaching heroes, I was a hungry and ambitious coach that wanted to rise to the top, just as we probably all have been in many shapes and forms. I was chasing after "The Big Time" and it took me to a lot of great places with a lot of great experiences. One of those great places being TCU coaching under coach

Franchione, and getting to coach a ton of talent like Hall of Famer Ladainian Tomlinson, and others like Aaron Schobel. I even got to coach in a couple bowl games with them. Along the chase I also met many wonderful coaching peers that I am still friends with to this day. But at some point I began to realize that my concept of the "Big time" may not have been so solid as I thought. The big time may not have really been as defined as I had liked to think. I stopped and took some time to ponder this concept and came up with an epiphany. This epiphany was that "not everybody's big time". What I meant by that was that on its surface, not everyone was meant to be a top level professional coach; in the case of football, an NFL level coach. Underneath this layer of epiphany I realized that "not everybody's big time" also meant that the term "Big time" was fluid. It could have many different definitions depending on who was seeking it. So how could one continue chasing "it" when "it" wasn't even really solidly pinned down and defined or possibly even tangible.

The only thing under these attributes; intangible, invisible, undefinable, that we can chase is God.

I recently watched one of my former players go into the NFL hall of fame. Ladainian Tomlinson of TCU, gave one of the greatest hall of fame induction speeches. It was a long speech with many great points, but the one big thing we took from that speech was his saying "Football is a microcosm of reality". He was saying that the game of football was a mirror image, a metaphor of life. And in football we're chasing an ultimate victory, mirrored in reality, that ultimate victory is accepting Christ. So L. T.'s speech also reminded me of another quote: "The Hall of Fame is only good as long as time shall be, but keep in mind, God's Hall of Fame is for eternity! To have your name inscribed up there is greater by far, than all the fame and all the praise of every man-made star!" - Author Unknown.

It is this thought process that led me to examine my own hall of fame chase. A danger for all up and coming coaches, is getting caught running on the loop of the "performance wheel". We live in a society that looks at social media profiles and paints an external, false image of what true success really is. Twenty years ago, if I took a photo, I would have had to have it developed and usually had no idea what the final product would fully look like. Today, we don't develop, we can take an image immediately, if not take hundreds immediately. If we don't get the image we like at first, we can use other apps to manipulate and transform ourselves into an image we so desire. Pastor Ben Daily said something that caught my attention in a counseling session. I was confessing my frustrations with coaching and the profession in general, and he had a perplexing response. Pastor Dailey told me, "Tony, every monday I write my resignation letter." I was blown away. He went on to tell me that every monday he would feel like what he did on sunday wasn't enough, and never would be enough. Therefore he'd contemplate quitting. It wasn't until he got a grasp of what he called his true gospel mission, the mission to lead people to a higher calling using his profession. See, he was stuck on the performance wheel, until he realized that it wasn't about how you performed. It was about something bigger. I think the same applies to us as coaches.

Ultimately, along with Frosty's teachings, I realized that it all led to the conclusion you MADE the "Big time" WHERE you're at. This whole path way down defining the big time was a humbling one and a process full of maturing. Have you gone down this path yourself? As mentioned before, ambition isn't bad or sinful in its nature. BUT if you let it drive you as your sole fuel for every decision made in your life then it borderlines an addiction. And I can tell you myself, chasing after this "Big Time" concept is like chasing a ghost. It's frustrating.

We're not saying don't dream. Quite the contrary. We're saying take the time now and figure out what exactly is the "Big Time" to you. Define it and find a solid dream that you can strive for instead of an abstract prestige. Herm Edwards once said, "I tell my players dreaming is ok, but when you wake up it's sometimes gone. I want my guys to have a vision, because vision leads to goals." Everyone should take the time to define and mediate their thoughts on what exactly their "Big time" is. Because depending on where you're at in life, your definition could and probably will change. As we get older we begin to cut away the superfluous fat of our lives and of our hearts desires as we begin to have our eyes opened to what really matters. In his book, "*Wins, Losses, and Lessons*" Lou Holtz writes, "...it's not *what* you have but *who* you have that counts. I had family, coaches, teachers, and friends who cared about me, and who took a strong interest in raising me well. Without those people, all the riches in the world would have meant nothing. Their love was all the wealth I needed."

How could you not think then, after this change, that your goals and dreams have changed as well. Change is ok, usually it's more than ok it's a good thing. This type of dream/goal change is good as well. But we cannot move on to becoming the best leader, the best shepherd if we haven't reconciled with our deepest desires career wise. If you're not aligned with what you want out of your job, then you won't be able to work efficiently and get the most out of the experience and more importantly; you won't be able to GIVE as much as you could during the experience. If you haven't taken the time yet, do it now. Take the time to humble yourself before God and realize what it is exactly you're chasing and WHY you're chasing it.

Chapter 6

Now, adding to the running theme of the whole conversation so far, how can we use this self analysis of our definition of dreams and the "big time" to help affect our team and players?

One primary thing I had to learn about this whole internal search was that you made the big time where you are at first. Treat yourself, your job, school and position like it's the end all be all in your mind first. When this is done it allows you to turn towards your team and players specifically. When examining our players, we must realize that we can't see one player as more "Big time" than the other; despite their starting position and despite their talents or coachability. As a coach we are all probably guilty of thinking this way at some time in our career. But you must realize that EVERY SINGLE player deserves to be coached, and deserves to be loved up. Now that's hard to do I know. Especially with the players that are "Resistant". Jeff Janssen has written a great book called the "Commitment Continuum" that every coach should check out. He also has a great website full of knowledge if you just search his name or the "Commitment Continuum". In the book though, Janssen breaks down the scale of a player's commitment to a team and your leadership as a coach. It's a stretched out continuum that at one end has fully "committed". At the other end, in red, is "Resistant". Those resistant kids; we all have them. The big issue comes up when your "leaders", or the kids that all the others look up to, are in the resistant section. Check out Janssen's stuff on how to get that issue resolved as well as other great lessons on creating a culture of commitment on your team.

But it's the resistant kids that need love and coaching too. You have to take a step back and look at today's society on how it judges boys. Usually, boys today are learning that they are judged on three things.

1. Their wallet size

2. Their sexual prowess

3. Their sports accolades

These are all material things that as we get older and become true men of character, we realize don't really describe you internally. At Least, I hope you know this. I hope you know that to be a "Man" you don't need any of these things. Chasing them, like chasing an undefined "Big Time", is like chasing ghosts. God is the ultimate Judge and he judges a person by far greater and less materialistic evidence.

We must be aware as coaches of the youth though that these things start to creep into the minds of our boys. Sometimes these things are not even vocalized, they are just learned subconsciously through the current culture. It's because of this that we must be good examples of what true manhood is and to know that, you have to seek it in yourself first. But on top of that, you must also be looking past the surface of a child's exterior and searching for the root cause. That "resistant" kid might be acting that way because of the pressures he's feeling in his world to have one of those three things listed above. Or maybe he's resistant to your coaching because he hears you preaching about striving to be more than those three things, but then hears you talking to your coaching buddies about having those three. We must be conscious of the ever changing judging lenses of society on our players because they feel that pressure. And everyone deals with pressure differently.

Ultimately, in turning inward you can begin to sidestep the ego. You can begin to define or redefine what exactly is "big time" for you in your life. Once you've figured these things out, you can now go and try to be the best example of manhood to your team. Strive to be in the now with ambition. Ambition isn't bad, but don't let it keep you locked in the future of your desires. Speak those desires and dreams and meditate on them when the time is allotted, but when it's time to be in the present, be there! And decide to make the big time where you're currently at.

Here are some things you can start doing now to help define/redefine your "Big time":

1. Figure out what matters now. In the present. Make a list of it all. While doing this be honest with yourself but realize a few things. You should look at family and a spouse (if you're married) and first think what's best for them out of your career decisions. Next, calm yourself if needed in realizing that you should have an appreciation for the system and the journey. If you're dying to leave where you're at and get onto the next job, be patient. Enjoy the now, enjoy the journey, and pay your dues. You're gaining valuable experience now and God has you there for a reason.

2. Make the Big time where you're at now. To start this process, take the time to list or speak your daily blessings. This helps reframe your mindset into a force of positivity. Therefore you'll be able to exude positivity but you're also going to be ATTRACTING positive outcomes. Another way to do this is take some time and

look back on what you've accomplished already, at different jobs. Let these accomplishments motivate you to keep going and reciprocate these triumphs in the job you're at now.

3. Part of any job, like mentioned before, is realizing that no kid is more big time than the other. To do this: you must realize that you are called to a higher purpose as a spiritual educator and leader. Colossians 3:23 reads, "Whatever you do, work at it with all your heart, as working for the Lord, not for human masters…" You should carry this mindset at all times and act as if there's someone who's always watching that can bless you. Let this move and influence your behavior. And, always try to remember that most of the time, kids need US (Coaches) more than we need them.

Fourth Quarter

The Train Stop

"Hope is not a strategy."
~ Lou Holtz

Chapter 7

Ilook around to all of my friends and family. I remember my teammates. I remember kids I have coached and are still currently coaching. Everyone is looking for purpose in their life. You need to realize today that there is purpose in being a coach. There's purpose in teaching a young man or woman how to become the best at a game. Because that game itself teaches so much about life. I know that's been said before but it's so true. The lessons on suffering, respecting authority positions, working, sacrifice, selflessness and collaborating with others, and just having the pressure of not wanting to let a team of people down; they all are reflections of the real world. As a coach, you have the possibility to make a huge impact on a young adult's life. You have the possibility to make thousands of impacts on thousands of lives (Depending on how long you coach). But that's just it: the ride does eventually stop. Unfortunately, sometimes your voice gets old and falls on deaf ears. Sometimes our body just doesn't hold up like it used to, and we gotta change our lifestyle. So how do you respond when the train stops, and you have to get off?

I believe that this transition is made the easiest far before it ever happens. If you put forth the effort to establish a foundation in your life that doesn't rest on selfish gains, materialistic accolades, or tangible whims, then you should be ok. IF you set out to build a foundation in God, then you'll know that when the train ride does stop, that your life is still in the hands of something far greater than you and I, and that you're just moving on to the next phase in His plan. One way to begin to help strengthen this foundation as a coach, is to start a coaches outreach or a coach's bible study. Your staff may already be doing one and you need to start going if so! The church was established for corporate fellowship. Christianity rests heavily on exceeding not only in personal growth with Christ but also in external social growth with Christ as a collective group. So as a coach, nothing changes. Your staff, or your friend group, should strive to be its own community of like minded followers all trying to help sharpen one another. On top of trying to create fellowship with like minded peers, you should be seeking a mentor type of relationship. Maybe that takes the form of a coach who's older than you, and who is actively everyday trying to exude a Christ-like lifestyle. These types of relationships are so beneficial. I think everyone, no matter their field or calling, should have a mentor that they can turn to in times required guidance. Remember:

"Coaching gives one a chance to be successful as well as SIGNIFICANT."
~ Lou Holtz

Hopefully you've learned a couple things from this read in regards to how much meaning and purpose you have as a coach. Despite how much time you may think you have before your train stops, there's always still time to begin working on the little things and becoming the best coach you can be. There's always still room for improvement as an efficient leader. And, part of being an example of manhood or womanhood, is continually striving to define and exude what manhood/womanhood is. Efficiency in life is a game that never stops. Your number one rival is the old you. You're racing with your current self. So fall in love with the game and compete your heart out.

We've compared coaching to the ministry of a pastor, but as we conclude there's another role in the church that is a lot like a coach as well. The first part of the word "Missionary" is "Mission". Like a Missionary, we as coaches must be "Mission-oriented".

This might be a word you've used in your program! But are you living it? Like a missionary, who goes out into parts of the world and spreads the good news while investing in a community, you must do the same as a coach. Invest, and spread the good word. Sometimes this message and mission is best carried out by simply acting the part. You don't always have to speak it to them. But before you set out for your mission trip, make sure you are prepared. Prepare inwardly, mentally, and spiritually everyday. Because as a coach, everyday you're going out into the mission field. Look at your position this way, and you'll surely impact lives. You might even save a few.

Overtime

Collection of Essays,
to bring home the Victory

When I finished writing this book, I realized there are many other voices that share this philosophy. Below is a collection of essays from various people within ministry, coaching and athletics in general, who felt the same way about ministry in coaching. This is just a handful of the many people that I've been blessed to cross paths with.

Being a Faith-Driven Leader

By Chris Melson

Athletic Coordinator, Head Coach

Mansfield Legacy High School

I am the by-product of two educators, my parents, Carl and JoLyn Melson. My mom taught elementary school for 34 years and my dad coached and taught for 41 years. I was raised in a home that centered around the local schools and specifically the high school athletic programs. My father was a head football and track coach in several small towns in Oklahoma and Texas. When I was 5 years old, I began roaming the sidelines as the ball boy where my #1 job was to get the kicking tee back to the sideline after each kickoff. I remember several times when the grass was so high, that I had to really scramble to find that sucker. I also rode the bus on many track meet trips that would start with me tagging along with my dad as early as 4am to go get the bus and getting home past midnight. I was totally exhausted, but totally thrilled to have spent the whole day with my dad and his athletes. It made me feel special and like I was a member of the team! The athletes my dad coached seemed larger than life...I wanted to be like them. As I grew older and saw how the athletes responded to my dad's motivation, I soon wanted to be just like my dad...my hero!

As I got into high school and began to excel on the field and in the classroom, my dream of playing at the University of Oklahoma became a reality. I graduated from Ada High School in Ada, OK. My senior year, we won the Class AAA State Championship and I graduated with a 4.0 GPA. I don't say that to sound braggadocious, but rather as a fact my parents would hold over me as I started my college education. My mom and dad both would tell me time and again, "Son, you are too smart to be a coach! Go do something where you can earn a lot of money and live in one place with your family!" I attended 4 different schools in 4 different towns my 1st 4 years of school. Kindergarten was spent in Sulphur, OK. I spent the 1st grade in Konawa, OK. We lived in Hobbs, NM my 2nd grade year. In the

3rd grade, we moved to Enid, OK...where we stayed until after my 7th grade year. So, when I had done so well in school, both my folks wanted me to go use my brain to make a more stable and lucrative living.

I decided to major in Business Management at Oklahoma. As I was set to graduate in the Spring of 1992, I had 3 really good job offers in the business world. As I contemplated which to choose, my heart was saying…." This is not what you want to do...this is not your desire. You need to be a coach like your dad!" I couldn't believe it. I just spent 5 years studying business so I could go make good money, but I couldn't deny God's spirit stirring inside my soul. I talked to my parents and shared that I felt God telling me to be a coach. I just couldn't find peace in my soul when I thought about doing anything else.

I had given my life to Christ when I was 13 years old at a summer youth camp. From that point on in my life, God has been an integral part of my everyday life. That summer, we moved from Enid to Ada. As we were moving into our home, a man named John O'dell helped us unload our U-Haul. John was the area representative working with the Fellowship of Christian Athletes. John and I quickly formed a strong bond through Christ and he began to disciple me in my faith. As I went through high school, John taught me to be bold in my faith. He had bible studies with me and my friends. He challenged us to memorize scripture and the importance of God's Word in the life of a Christian. He truly discipled me. I have always felt that he was like the Apostle Paul and I was like his Timothy.

The week before 8th grade football practice was to begin, my father took me up to Ada Middle School to meet my new coaches. The coaches office was barely an office, more like a lobby outside of a restroom shoved into the far hallway in the West gym. As I entered the office, I was introduced to the head coach, Jim Cooper. He asked me a question and I answered, "Yeah." Wrong answer! He barked at me like no man ever had, "Yes Sir!" I replied back, voice shaking, "Yes Sir." So began our relationship.

That 8th grade year, Coach Cooper barked at me and my new teammates on a daily basis. If he thought you were being soft, he would call you a 'haircomber'. I'm not sure what that meant, but I knew it was not good! He believed that we would be the best conditioned team each game. We ran a LOT for 8th graders. Coach Cooper demanded that we do things exactly the way he and his staff instructed. There was no other way, just the way we had been taught. He believed, and he was correct, that if we all do our jobs the way we had been taught to and do it with great effort, we would be successful. Jim and his staff of Wade Evans, Buddy Staggs and Mike Whitson took a bunch of 8th graders who had never played organized football in their lives (except for me, I had played since 3rd grade in Enid), and led us to Ada's first undefeated 8th grade team since 1961...it was now 1982. His passion and demanding spirit caused us to really dislike him at first, in fact, many of us would say we hated him that year. But as time passed and we entered high school, we all admired and respected him, especially me! I always have needed to be challenged and pushed hard. That is when I excel. Jim Cooper did that for me and my teammates.

After our senior football season had ended in a 34-17 victory in the State Championship on Lewis Field on the campus of Oklahoma State University, my teammates and I celebrated with our friends and family on the turf for around 20 minutes. As I was leaving the field to go get changed in the locker room, Coach Cooper was standing at the tunnel waiting for me. He stuck out his hand and congratulated me. I thanked him. He then said something that I didn't expect and never will forget. He said, "you know it's not over." I said, "excuse me. We just won, it's over coach, we are State Champs!" He said, "You are right the season is over, but now you have a responsibility." I'm thinking, "what?" He said, "it is now up to you to come back and teach other players how to do what you and your teammates have accomplished." Of course he challenged me...that is just who he is. He basically said that I needed to be a coach and teach other kids how to be champions. I said, "sure coach" and headed to the locker room..

So, as I graduated from OU in May of 1992 with a Business degree, the desire of wanting to be like my father and accepting the challenge Coach Cooper had given me as an 18 year old kid, I decided to be a high school football coach. I went to East Central University in Ada and got my teaching certificate and became a coach for Ada. It felt like it was my calling. God had used 3 influential men in my life to get me to this point; My dad, John O'dell and Jim Cooper. As I entered the coaching profession, I felt that coaching would be my ministry. I would coach to influence young people for the Lord. I would challenge them and motivate them like my dad and Coach Cooper did me and I would share my faith with them like John O'Dell had taught me to. That is exactly what I began doing in the Fall of 1992... and have been tremendously blessed ever since in my career!

I spent 4 years in Ada as an assistant under my high school coach, Larry McBroom. He is amazing as a person and coach. Besides the men mentioned earlier, Larry had the next biggest impact on me. He is the best coach I have ever seen or been around. He is the consummate encourager and like Cooper, demanded the best out of me on a daily basis. He shared his Christian faith with us and it was obvious what he believed in and he modeled that for staff and players, alike. We won 40 games in a row from 1993 to 1995 along with 3 consecutive State Championships.

After my 4th year with Larry, he took a job in Weatherford, TX and I took a job as an assistant football coach and the head girls track coach in Rockwall, Texas. I spent 9 years in those roles working for 2 different men. Paul Potter for the first 2 years and Mark Elam for the next 7 years. Paul was a transplant for Oklahoma who had been successful at Edmond High School. He struggled at Rockwall and was let go after my 2nd season with him. He had a heart of gold and cared deeply about his players and coaches. Mark Elam came from North Mesquite where he had been extremely successful. I learned so much from Coach Elam. He was the most organized football coach I had worked for. He had things planned down to the exact minute for weeks on end. He coached kids extremely hard and demanded them to be tough and play hard, and they did! He had a HUGE heart for people, although from the outside, he seemed rough and at times resembled a 'wild-man'. I learned many great things from being his assistant. Although we coached hard and coached well, in the 9 years I served as an assistant in Rockwall, the football team never qualified for the playoffs.

As it is with any job and being under any boss, you learn some things you would do if you were head coach and some things you would do differently. The one thing I really wanted for the players on all the teams I had coached was for them to hear the unashamed, bold declaration of the TRUTH about Jesus. I felt like a lot of the messages coaches were giving to players were to get them through a tough workout or a tough game or a tough day, but nothing eternal. I would hear this year's motto is....but what are we really about? Things like, "One More in '94" "Jacket Fight Never Dies." "Tiger Pride" "Just Do It" "One Heartbeat" Some of the ones I see today are things such as, "Row the Boat" "Pull the Rope" "Hold the Line"

To me, something was missing. There's got to be more. I wanted players to hear TRUTH from God's word. Although I shared my faith with my position players, it was hard to get that message to permeate over an entire program when you are not the leader.

So, the desire God gave me after a couple years in Rockwall was to become the Head Football Coach of my own program. It was not so I could call better plays or run this offense or that. No, it was to set the course of the entire program based on biblical truths from the Word of God. I wanted the young men under my supervision to walk out of the field house their senior year to know 3 things: God made you special and for a purpose, Hard Work is Valuable and Jesus Christ is your only hope. I wanted to give them the TRUE keys to joy, peace and prosperity not only in this life, but the life eternal.

I began applying for head coaching jobs at the age of 34. My wife, Judy and I, would pray over every application we filled out and mailed in. I had applied for 38 jobs and been turned down for everyone. On try number 39, we finally got our prayer answered. At the age of 37, I was offered my 1st head football coaching job, and I accepted. It was in Electra, Texas. Electra is a very small school located half-way between Wichita Falls and Vernon on Highway 287. In 2005, it had an enrollment of 154 kids in the high school. We were class AA. I had no assistants to take with me, but an old friend of mine had just retired from Oklahoma and was looking to get back into coaching and double dip. His name was Coach Cooper. He came with me...it was a god send! We spent 2 years in Electra and established early the things we wanted to teach...Be Unselfish, Little Better Everyday. I felt these two principles were biblical and had scripture to back each one of them up. I felt they were easily relatable to football and being a good teammate.

> Philipians 2:3, *"Do nothing out of selfish ambition or vain conceit. Rather, in Humility value others above yourselves.*
>
> Phillippians 3:14, *"I press on toward the goal to win the prize."*

I would share scripture on a weekly basis and tell the players that they were special and that I loved them. To say this was a culture shock to this community would be a huge understatement. These kids and their families were used to coaches cursing and ruling with an iron fist. I wanted to represent Christ for these kids and coach with an eternal purpose. We ended up having a really good year and made the playoffs before losing in the 1st round to perennial power, Canadian.

We had a lot of good players coming back next year and we dropped down to Class A. We were pre-season ranked #6 in the state. Huge expectations for a 2nd year coach. We lost the 1st game of the year to rival Holiday, 7-6. They were AA. We lost to Class

AA Childress, Paradise after that and then played poorly at Class A Valley View and started off 0-4. My superintendent shared with me that the next few games were really important...I was like, no joke. The parents held an impromptu booster meeting trying to ambush me and get me flustered, but I just shut that down and told them we were going to have a good season, just be patient. I didn't want to leave the house, the whole town was talking about firing me, how I was too soft. I had a mom come to me after practice that week and let me know that the boys needed me to curse them out, not preach to them. She said they need a coach not a preacher. I assured her that I would not be cussing out any players and that I was going to be myself and she just needed to relax. I dove head first into the Book of Psalm during this trying time. This was tough for my whole family. I told my wife that no matter what the scoreboard said, we were winning each day because God's word was being shared and I truly believed that.

Game #5 was our homecoming game. I had scheduled a private school out of Ft. Worth called Ft. Worth Christian. We really did need a win, I was hoping and praying for a homecoming celebration, not a funeral procession. I want to stress that I had drawn a tremendous amount of peace from God through His word and the Psalms. When the other team got off their charter bus, I was like, "OH MY, they look good." I was right. At halftime, we were trailing 27-6. Ouch! The boo-birds were out and very vocal as I walked toward the locker room. It was at this very moment that I felt God was speaking to me through his Holy Spirit. He was telling me what to say to my players and how to respond to them at halftime. He basically told me to go into the locker room, brag to my players, tell them that they were a great group of kids and that something good was fixing to happen. He said to tell them they were really close to doing great things. He said to tell them they were going to win 28-27! So, I gathered my staff in my office and shared with them exactly what I felt God had impressed on my heart to share with our team. That is exactly what I did.

We kicked off to start the 2nd half. The 1st play from scrimmage, their tailback went 80 yards for a touchdown…...but, it was called back due to a penalty. They never scored again! With 16 seconds left on the clock, we scored to make the score 26-27. We just needed to go for 2 and make it and we would win 28-27! I called timeout and talked to my players on the sideline. We decided to run a halfback pass. We would toss it to our tailback and he would run a few steps then throw a comeback to my all-state wide receiver in the corner of the endzone. As we break the huddle from the sideline and go line up, we are penalized for having 12 men on the field. So we get backed up 5 yards and I call another time out. As we are debating on the sideline, I told my team we were going to kick it and win in overtime. My tailback, the wild-man on the team, DJ Wyatt, said, "Come on coach, live a little! I'll get the ball to Greg and we will win 28-27 just like you said." I said, 'you got it..let's do it." We ran it and the kids executed it perfectly and we won 28-27. As I walked off the field I couldn't quit smiling. One of my players came up to me and said, "Coach, we won 28-27, just like you said we would." I nodded and said, "isn't amazing what God can do!" That started a great run by my team and we ended up getting beat in the 4th round of the playoffs. I didn't have to cuss, I just tried to honor HIm with all I was doing! He blessed us!!

That January (2007), I applied for the head coaching position for a school that was being built in Mansfield, TX...Legacy High School. By the grace of God, I was granted an interview and 2 days later offered the job at a brand new 5A school in the metroplex! Amazing Grace!! I had never been anywhere that was brand new, with no tradition, no past troubles, no past successes, nothing. I was going to get to build a program from the ground up from scratch. This was a golden opportunity to base a program completely on God's Word and It's principles. I attended a leadership seminar that spring and heard Eddie Debartolo, Jr. speak. He shared that any organization needed core values and a mission statement that encompassed those values to drive the organization and create the culture for success. Wow...that was it...that was what I needed in order to build this program. So, I prayed and thought and prayed some more about what our core values needed to be for the Legacy football program.

After a few weeks of deliberation I settled on the following Core Values: Team, Hard Work, Truth, Relationships, Championships, Today and Future. We would value these 7 things and they would drive how we do what we do with our team. Each with a Bible Verse reference: Team (Ecclesiastes 4:12), Hard Work (Prov. 14:23), Truth (John 14:6), Relationships (Phillipians 2:3), Championships (I Cor. 9:24), Today (Psalm 118:24), Future (Jeremiah 29:11). The Mission Statement reads: Our Mission is - Winning Championships based on the Relationships we build with our Team as we Work Hard, Today, for our Future! This is a Truth statement. So, I had signs made with all 7 values and our logo on each. They were posted in every locker room in our field house above the lockers. They have now been there for 14 years. The Mission Statement is the hallway and the entrance to the Varsity locker room. This has provided our program with a consistent message and drives our culture. It will never change.

With the foundation laid, each year we teach our players the meaning of each value, the biblical basis for each one and have them memorize the Mission Statement. It allows a great segway into our philosophy on how to teach our players how to be successful in this life and the life eternal. Players hear scripture on a regular basis from their coaches on a weekly, if not, daily basis. The most prominent verse they hear is Proverbs 14:23 - "All hard work produces a profit, but mere talk leads to poverty." It is a core value they hear again and again and I would say 99% of the players can recite it by memory when they leave our program.

I constantly look for scripture to apply to our current situation in season and out of season. God's Word is not empty or shallow. It is powerful and useful for teaching and correction. It will never change and will never let you down. I model that and share that on a genuine basis, because ultimately, I will be held accountable for the time and opportunity I had here on earth with these young men. I will have to answer to the Lord on what I did with this time...he won't ask me how many games did you win, how many titles, etc. Although, that is very important to me and to our program! I am as fierce as a competitor as you will ever find. I teach I Cor. 9:24 to all my players and coaches. God declares we should all, "RUN TO WIN." We are not called to run to participate, but to WIN! God demands our best! You won't find anywhere in His Word that you are to do anything half-hearted. In fact, God always tells us to do everything as hard as you can and with ALL your heart! Like Jim Cooper, God demands our best, always!! I teach Colossians 3:23 to drive this home…." Whatever you do, do it with ALL your heart as working for the Lord and not for man." That is a HIGH standard and what I demand from my players and coaches. It is what God demands…I love that!

I have heard coaches say that they prepare their players for 'life after football'. That is a good thing, but scripture tells us that this life is just a mist, a vapor (James 4:14). What I feel God has put on my heart is to prepare young men for 'life after death'. I share with my players after each season that my hope and prayer is that I will see their faces in heaven. That is how I will determine if we have been successful in our program…did the players find salvation in Jesus. That is a high standard, I know…but it is what God desires and is what I desire. Because of this desire burning inside of me, I constantly look for ways to incorporate the Bible with our players…

mainly the need for Jesus as their savior. I've never thought of myself as a coach who is a Christian, but a Christian who coaches. I can say that in the past 15 years of being a head coach, God has blessed us with some great winning seasons and some not so good ones. We have been 12 - 3 and we have been 1 - 9. However, whether or not we are winning on the scoreboard, we can win by consistently sharing the truth of God's word. The one constant in our program is that our players hear the same message year in and year out. There is no gimmick or motto, just the basic fundamental truths found in God's Word. The program is built and re-established each year with our Core Values and Mission Statement.

These are some of the reasons I feel that I am a faith-driven leader. My faith permeates in every aspect of my life and our football program. I don't know how a person can really follow Christ and that not be the case. It is a natural expression of the grace God has given me expressed in my profession. I truly love the Lord and love my players and coaches. I am so thankful for the men in my life... Carl Melson, John O'dell and Jim Cooper, who influenced me to be a Christian who coaches. My family has been blessed in this profession and I can't wait to get to heaven to see how we really did!

"Why Sports?"

By Tommy Nelson

Senior Pastor

Denton Bible Church

Former QB for University of North Texas

Have you ever wondered why sports exploded into our culture in the 20th century? Why not in the 300 years earlier?

The 20th century was our country's movement from rural to urban life. From the country to the city. From the farm to the factory. With that movement, fathers were now separated from the family and child rearing duties fell upon the mothers. Without the farm, there is little place for boys to join in the responsibility of work. Out of that phenomenon, and that of immigration, boys began to find support in gangs, both of neighborhoods and nationalities. As a result, the term "juvenile delinquency" was coined as boys were disconnected from culture.

The solution? YMCA, boys club, youth groups, Boy Scouts, the military dash – team sports. Coaches became the priests and pastors of the 20th century. They were the men that boys now connected with.

As a matter of fact, there was such a concern among college presidents that football was surpassing education that a special gathering of college presidents was called to discuss the problem. At that meeting the greatest football coach of the day, Knute Rockne, addressed the presidents. He said that with World War One over there would be no need for a military (so he thought) and with urbanization a boy would not know the responsibility of a job. The church and the home had become matriarchal. The one place where a young man could find a prelude to life would be football (baseball and basketball had not yet arisen in high schools and colleges). The new priest was the coach. For the sake of young men, football had to continue. Coaches held the key to the men of the future.

Rockne was right. He still is.

Coaching beyond the field

By Lewis Caralla

Head Strength Coach

Georgia Tech

Being a coach is truly a special opportunity to help others. It gives you a platform to make a difference in someone's life unlike any other. Being a great coach tends to always get confused by the amount of wins you have during your career. That's exactly the opposite reason of why you should get into coaching.

I've been a strength and conditioning coach for the past 13 years and have worked at 9 different division one schools. The sport I've always worked with was football. It's been a blessing to play the game my entire life and to now still be involved as a coach. The reason I wanted to be a strength and conditioning coach was the simple fact the I love football, but I love the work that goes into it much more. Having had the privilege of coaching so many different players across this country the past decade has given me great insight of what coaching is really about.

Every player I've ever coached, I've interviewed first. The goal was to learn everything possible about that individual so I could do my very best to impact his life. The interview is always my favorite part of the job because it teaches you things that you couldn't possibly know if you never asked. The simplest questions sometimes turned into the deepest answers that they were waiting to get off their chest. I believe it's one of the most impactful things I've done as a coach to get on the same page as the players from the start.

I've always told every player I've ever coached that I was never there to be their friend, I was there to be their best friend. Because their best friend knows what they really want. He knows when they're being average and coasting. He knows what they've been through to even have this opportunity. He can read body language and isn't quick to make rash judgements. He calls you out when you need it. But most importantly, he's always there for you when you need him. A friend might let you coast and settle into average because it makes him feel better about himself.

I also believe as a coach that it should be mandatory to share positive and encouraging messages to your players on a daily basis. After every lift group or run day, I've always given the team a message before they leave. The messages consist of quotes, stories, mistakes, flaws, potential, adversity, faith, commitment, etc. I believe if you share your heart with the players, their heart is what you'll get. The most common thing the players I coached years ago always mention is the fact that they miss those messages. They don't miss the wins. There's so much more to being a coach then people realize.

I truly believe that the greatest impact you'll ever have as a coach is the impact you'll never see. Do they get the great job after graduation? Do they become incredible husbands and fathers one day? Do they have a competitive spirit that they can always take with them? Are they self-driven? Do they have great habits and discipline to always fall back on when they don't get their way? Do they always feel in their heart they can reach out to you at any point? Is their memory of you one of the best memories they have in their life? These are all things that only time will tell. One thing's for sure, the time you have with your athletes will expire. But the one thing that never has to expire is the impact you had in their lives.

If coaching was just about winning, I wouldn't want to be a coach. When you're given the keys to the hearts and souls of the players you coach, it's special. Don't take it for granted. Be a coach beyond the field because in the end, it's all that matters.

Rise

Steven Greek

Head Football Coach/Associate A.D.

Liberty Christian High School,

Argyle, Texas

> **"Do not rejoice over me, O my enemy.**
> **Though I fall will rise; Though I dwell**
> **in darkness, the Lord is a light for me."**
> Micah 7:8

Leadership is tough.

In the profession of coaching we believe tough people win. We believe adversity can be a friend. We believe that working through struggle is where championship culture and programs are built on and off the field. Victories and championships are sweet and losses are difficult. But somewhere, right in the middle of the mess, we find a ministry of significance and impact like no other.

Leadership is hard.

Leadership is hard enough when everything is going great. We cast vision, build the blueprint, mentor, listen, encourage, duplicate, delegate, oversee, manage, guide, direct, redirect, counsel, instruct and discipline. Throw in adversity and leadership gets very interesting to say the least. Experience a loss, take a dip in the rankings, upset a player, parent, or coworker...and problems can pile on.

Leadership is rewarding.

Seeing an individual accomplish something they once thought impossible is priceless. Being part of a team that learns to believe, battle, and overcome - creates memories and bonds for life. Seeing a person who comes from brokenness and dysfunction be transformed is amazing. The faith, unity and family atmosphere that can be experienced in the right kind of culture, team, business, and relationship is so life changing, that once experienced, the desire to live with such purpose and passion in all areas of life becomes so rewarding.

Leadership matters.

If everyone could lead...everyone would. "Monday Morning Quarterbacks" are everywhere fighting for a voice of significance. They second guess everything. They accuse: "They should've... They could've... If I were in charge I would… (Simply fill in the blank)." Anonymous letters, Twitter Trolls and social media experts aim to set the record straight. They can't wait for you to make a mistake, to run your name through the mud. It makes them feel good. But it only reveals who they are as a person. Typically someone so miserable with themselves and their own life, that they can't at the very least hold their tongue. The values of support, trust, uphold, and encouragement are foreign to them. They want to "run it" or "ruin it" - and they don't really care which it is. Infighting, pride, ego, disappointment, and unmet expectations can destroy good relationships. Enough of these ingredients and we have the recipe for disaster. Darts get thrown. Arrows come at leaders from all directions. Enemies on the outside. Enemies Within. Friendly Fire might be what beats us up the most. Division is the tool of the devil. Unfortunately, this is common.

Disfunction in our culture is so much of "normal" society. It's no wonder it bleeds over into the locker room and the office. It's in sports, marriages, families, business, churches, and society. As the disease of "me" runs wild across the land, there are the right kind of leaders, with the right kind of focus, and the right kind of purpose and energy whose sole purpose is to make a difference and impact lives in the things that matter. There are leaders who want to create belief, unity, and strength. Where "We" comes before "Me". Where serving one another brings purpose and strength...and relationships deeper than most will ever experience in their life.

And this is why "Significant Leadership" is so desperately needed. We are called to change what is normal. It starts with us. The person in the mirror. Those we call family. We cannot give what we do not possess. We are called to resist the status quo. As we grow we glow. And as we glow we go. We are called to "Rise" up, grow in faith, aspire higher, become more, and develop and multiply ourselves. We are called to be a light in the darkness. This is a calling. This is the challenge. This is why leadership matters.

We also must learn to surrender the outcome. In leadership we want results. But we don't always see the results right away. It may show up on the scoreboard and in the Win-Loss column. It may not. But that doesn't diminish the work or the impact. We can lead the right way with the right focus, right energy, right motives. This does not guarantee victory in all areas. Some plant. Some water. God causes the growth. We just need to learn to keep the faith, show up, and do the work. I believe we will win - and help others to learn to win - in the things that matter most.

There is a time and season to everything and every phase of life. As leaders, may we learn to be thankful for each day, every opportunity to impact and shape lives, and enjoy the journey because it goes by fast.

I would like to share with you the vision, goals, and blueprint our leaders are building for the upcoming year. It is amazing to guide, develop and observe young leaders who want to see this walked out in their own lives, family, and team. I pray this may inspire you and those you lead in the days ahead:

Passion

- ✅ Play With Heart & Fiery Passion
- ✅ Hold each other Accountable
- ✅ Build Each other up
- ✅ Dive into it
- ✅ Lead By Example

"Therefore encourage one another and build one another up, just as you are doing." 1 Thessalonians 5:11

Action

- ✅ Be About It
- ✅ Faith, Family, Football
- ✅ Speak through Actions
- ✅ Do The Little Things Great
- ✅ Go Full Speed In Everything

"Little children, let us not love in word or talk but in deed and in truth." 1 John 3:18

Purpose

- ✅ Know Your Purpose & Identity IN CHRIST
- ✅ Embrace your Role for THE TEAM
- ✅ Take Pride in your role for THE TEAM
- ✅ Keep the Main Thing the Main Thing
- ✅ Build and Strengthen the COMMUNITY

"Trust in the Lord with all your heart, and do not lean on your own understanding. In all your ways acknowledge him, and he will make straight your paths." Proverbs 3:5-6

"Rise up; this matter is in your hands. We will support you, so take courage and do it." Ezra 10:4

Ministering to an athlete who is a non-believer... Counseling an athlete through a difficult time.

Rick LaFavers

Head Football Coach/A.D.

Ridgepoint High School,

Houston, Texas

I have often wished I had a better "testimony" to share with people and especially my athletes. I have thought how much easier it would be to relate and share an experience of my own to better connect with people sometimes. The "old come to Christ in the jail cell" or some other redemptive testimony that would make for a great movie and story to share. But see I really don't have that. I have been a Christian since I was a young child. I was raised in a Christian home with two parents that loved me and my sister and made sure we went to church every Wednesday and twice on Sundays. But this is not truly what planted the seed deep in my heart to care for and minister to my athletes who may be non-believers and help counsel my athletes through difficult times. My father was a high school athletic trainer and coach and I was able to witness him through his actions and observe my parents care for and reach out to athletes while I was growing up as a young child. My dad would often randomly pay for people's tabs before the whole Starbucks drive through pay it forward trend ever began. He would never let anybody pay for anything. Anytime people tried to argue, he would always respond with, "don't rob me of a blessing." We always had athletes over to our house for FCA and Bible studies. I was able to see first hand my mom and dad pour into those athletes and love them and share with them their Faith. I witnessed many athletes turn their life over to Christ while I was growing up. I never felt bold in "witnessing" and ministering because I thought I really don't have a "testimony." But as I have gotten older (and wiser), God has shown me and reminded me that I don't have to be like Paul and have some extraordinary testimony to minister and help my student athletes. I just need to make sure my athletes see Jesus in me. Like Moses I often struggle with what to say. I think to myself, "what am I supposed to say to this person?" "How can I help them?" I fear I don't have anything "profound" enough to truly make a difference and truly minister or comfort. I wish I had words like Inky Johnson or Tony Evans or any other great speaker who seems to have just the right thing to say at the right time. But God has shown me over the years if I will just get out of the way and let Him lead and humble myself and allow Him to work through me that is all the testimony I need because it isn't about me, it is about Christ in me. I have been able to see some seeds grow and have had more opportunities to minister and care for my student-athletes. When Tony and I spoke about topics to write about for this book, he suggested I write on this topic of ministering to non-believers and counseling my athletes through difficult times. I said "Tony this is probably the most difficult for me to write about" (just like Moses). But Tony kept encouraging me and reminded me of a time back when a great mutual friend and brother in Christ shared with Tony about he wouldn't be a Christian and wouldn't be going to Heaven if it wasn't for Rick LaFavers. I was definitely taken back from this comment, because I truly don't remember "witnessing" to this guy, who happened to be my college roommate/teammate at TCU. But he met Tony years down the road and shared that story with him. I was blown away. But it reinforced and strengthened my Faith in that as long as we truly connect and build relationships with people and let Christ in us shine through our actions and speech then God will do the rest. We just have to make sure we are ready to be used and are consistent. What my friend, Ashby, was able to witness was trying to live my life consistently for Christ. I fail every day, but it is the authenticity that I think helps connect and bridge the gap. Since graduating college and going on to coach I have had many athletes come through and I still struggle with the right thing to say or oftentimes how to share the gospel. But God still shows up each and every time during these "Moses moments" and seems to give me what I believe are the right words or actions. I had one particular athlete that was going through such a tragic and difficult time. His father had killed his mother and then walked out in front of a semi-truck and killed himself. His life came shattering down. I had never experienced anything remotely close or been around anything like this before. But God showed up. All I could do was love him and show him I loved him. I was there for him. It was through my consistent actions and how I lived and spoke and shared my own Faith that allowed a deep bond and trust to develop and he became like an adopted son to me. As I reflect back on my life thus far and the athletes I have been blessed to coach and be around, I recall and remember so many moments where I struggled for the right words but later discovered God's work and plan. So many times it isn't about having the right words or the right scripture to quote at a moment's notice. We as coaches have to understand and believe that God will and does use us if we allow Him to. I have many times just simply said to an athlete, "can I pray with/for you." Just these simple actions and words is all God needs. Just like any coach I love to win, but when it's all said and done, God doesn't care how many wins we have or how many championships we have. I want to make sure my athletes and staff see Christ and understand the love and peace in Christ. I want to live authentically so that they know it isn't always easy. It isn't blessings and happiness all the time. That Christians struggle and go through hardships. That the devil wants to kill, steal, and destroy. What I want my athletes to know is that in Christ there is comfort, healing, and joy. We just have to make sure as coaches they see that in our lives and in our daily routine! My hope and prayer for all of us is that we pray for opportunities to share our Faith and the Gospel. That we pray God opens doors and that our eyes and ears and hearts are sensitive enough to recognize those "moments." But what we fail to realize is that we are always being watched and observed. It is in these "uneventful" moments we must be consistent in our love and action and make sure people see Christ. That is how seeds are planted. To me that is how you minister daily to your athletes and that is how ultimately you can comfort and counsel them through difficult times because they see and believe and trust in you...the coach! Sometimes this is all the Jesus they see or know. We as coaches/leaders must Live out our Faith...Make Him known!

Anonymous NFL Agent

When I was asked to write this essay for Tony Johnson's book, I eagerly said yes. Almost without thinking I volunteered my writing skills and my deep encompassing John MacArthur or Tony Evans like knowledge of the written word. Reader, now is not the time for eye rolling and shaking of heads in disgust. I legitimately thought that I had something profound to say that would ultimately rival the aforementioned theological giants while shaking the foundations of the incomparable C.S. Lewis for good measure. At some point my ego faded, reality set in and I set myself to writing something that was spirit led and was sound enough spiritually to be tucked away, hidden and only to be revealed by the...

Guy on the end of the bench, by a writer unknown.

Tony's sub title, "The Pastoral Ministry of a Coach," immediately reminded me of the many times that I have been preached to, told in random conversation, or read somewhere that football was so much like the game of life. However, as I talked to coach Johnson and began to know his heart and listen to his testimonies, I knew that this journey of his would be impactful well beyond the well worn and mundane and overworked cliches of life and the game.

There are so many times that we think about the diamonds in the rough or the already physically desirable athletes that trot out onto a practice field and turn everyone's head. The guys that the coaches immediately think to themselves, "I can win with that guy" or "he's a stud," the efficacy goes on and on. We forever hear the tales of the guy that did not play High school football but now is a first round draft pick or the guy who played classic piano, got bored and started throwing 50 yard effortless strikes and is on his way to being the next Joe, Namath, Montana, Burrow? Those stories excite us and inspire countless numbers of young athletes and cause many coaches to scour their communities in search of that special "One!" But when I give spiritual thought to what it means to be a coach in ministry I think about those individuals that nobody wants. The broken, the uncoordinated, the little guy. If you're Nick Saban, you never even look for a guy like that. If you coach at a major power house Texas 6A or 5A program, you run those guys off quickly or encourage them to carry the water or keep the stat book.

But what exactly is ministry? It is simply really, it is giving your best effort to tell others about the awesome gift of Salvation found only by accepting Jesus Christ as one's Lord and Savior. And the good news is that Jesus gave us the perfect example on how to do this. He chose the little guy. The ones that no one wanted. The brothers Zebede, James and John, and the brothers Peter and Andrew were fishermen. Simple, not well educated, not well thought of, not super rich, heck they probably didn't smell good either, but these men of little regard were his first round picks and ultimately became his best friends. Jesus wasn't looking for speed or strength, he was looking for eager hearts, guys with the "put me in coach" spirit, men who were more concerned with what the Kingdom could get out of them than what the World could give to them. Throughout Jesus' life and ministry he coached others on how to live, treat others and advance God's kingdom and he almost always did so with those that the world had so little regard for. Fisherman, tax collectors, blind men, women (the implications here are huge considering how women were regarded during his time on earth), the sick, the diseased, the poor, children, societal rejects, you name it! But when Jesus wanted to put someone in the game he almost always looked at the end of the bench and got the most out of whoever was willing to give it.

Coaches, although you all want to win, remember that not every one of the young men and women you coach will go on to be Flo Jo or Tom Brady and in reality the best that you can hope for for many of them athletically is that they get to college on scholarship. The most important thing, as Christian men and women, is to put people in the game. Evidence by the way that you live, coach and treat others that Christ's team is worth being on. Look at the guys and gals who are not that great on the field as opportunities for them to be great on the field of Ministry and kingdom advancement.

Often times when we see depictions or think of Jesus, he is staring into the heavens, doe-eyed, prim and proper, handsome and dreamy, but the truth about Jesus' appearance as prophesied in the book of Isaiah was that "...There was nothing beautiful or majestic about his appearance, nothing to attract us to him. He was despised and rejected— a man of sorrows, acquainted with deepest grief. We turned our backs on him and looked the other way. He was despised, and we did not care." Isaiah 53:2-3 NLT. We would all do well to remember that as we coach in this game of Life. He Paid it all. Tony thank you so much for allowing me to contribute to this most noble of projects. May God bless it and you beyond measure.

Pastor Kareem Hickman

Associate Pastor

Calvary Church

Irving, Texas

The word "Coach" carries an enormous amount of weight in our culture. Coaches are respected and honored on the practice fields of historical high schools in rural towns in the deep south and on the courts of underfunded gyms in Chicago. Both places are filled with young men and women who have dreams to succeed and live above their present condition and surroundings, they are willing to put in the work that could change the course of their families. Both extremes carry their own differences, challenges and obstacles but there is one similarity, one common denominator that carries power and influence in each scenario. There is one icon that students from each extreme trust enough to follow and surrender their dreams to, it's a coach!

Too often we read of coaches who have used their influence to control, condemn and compensate. Very rarely do we hear of coaches who actually care for their students' success and well being more than their own. Coach Tony is committed to use his influence and power to point young men to a higher power. Students who are broken are introduced to a healer, students who are lost are introduced to a Good Father who will never leave them or forsake them, students who are convinced that they are a failures because of a goal that they did not achieve discover that they are loved and that their identity is not based on their activity but on an unconditional love that was demonstrated for all of us. Our culture has shifted, most students don't have a pastor to make these life changing introductions but every school has a coach. How great is it to have a coach who listens to God on behalf of his players. Thank you coach for being a vessel of honor, a light shining in the darkness, a voice carrying God's heart for this generation.

Mike Redwine, Ed.D.

Executive Vice President

Southern Nazarene University

Former College Head Football Coach

> **"...You're here to be light, bringing out the God-colors in the world. God is not a secret to be kept."** (Matthew 5:14, MSG)

It was January, 2000 and the American Football Coaches Association annual convention had just concluded. The meetings were in Anaheim, California that year so I decided to extend my stay so that I could go see one of our current players, Marvin Morris. Because we were between semesters, he was at his parent's home in San Diego for the holidays.

Marvin, a junior college transfer running back, had just completed his junior season year at MidAmerica Nazarene University, where I was serving as head coach. His father was serving in the military and the family lived on the base at Camp Pendleton. Because of the distance from our campus, his parents had not been able to attend a game and I had never had the opportunity to meet them. So, I rented a car, drove from Anaheim to their San Diego home and spent several hours getting to know Marvin's family.

By then it was early evening, so Marvin and I decided to have dinner together at a nearby restaurant. The meal and conversation were great. Our female server, most likely in her early 20's, provided excellent service and the conclusion of our meal, she asked me a series of interesting questions. Her first question was, "Are you a pastor?" To which I politely smiled and responded, "No."

She followed up with a second question, "Are you a youth pastor?" Once again, I replied, "No, I'm not a youth pastor."

Determined to guess my occupation, the young restaurant employee continued her inquiry. "Marriage counselor?", she asked. Chuckling, I responded, "No… and Mrs. Redwine would think that was hilarious!"

I informed her that the attempts at guessing my occupation were much closer than she might think and told her that in my profession, I had the chance to do all of those jobs and many more. Curiously, she asked, "So, what do you do?" I replied, "I am a football coach."

It took the questions from a young server at a restaurant in San Diego to remind me about what was most important about my coaching assignment. That I had the awesome responsibility of speaking truth and hope into the lives of hundreds of young men. That I had the privilege of being a listener and cheerleader as they unpacked their hopes and dreams. That I indeed, have the opportunity of wearing the "hat" of pastor, counselor, career mentor, academic tutor, financial advisor, and more.

Admittedly, I often felt inadequate as a coach and even less equipped to provide answers or advice in these important areas, especially when the occasion required providing spiritual counsel. I'm certain it was because I knew my personal shortcomings, but I'm convinced that this is when God does his best work. In 2 Corinthians 12:9 Paul writes, "But he (the Lord) said to me, 'My grace is sufficient for you, for my power is made perfect in weakness.' Therefore I will boast all the more gladly about my weaknesses, so that Christ's power may rest on me." (NIV) Fortunately, these interactions were more about listening and less about providing any answers or solutions. It was also comforting to know that God was available to join our conversation through the presence of his Holy Spirit.

So whether you are a Pastor, Youth Pastor, Marriage Counselor, Coach, or All of the Above, live into Matthew 5:14 (MSG) which states, "...God is not a secret to be kept." The challenge to you and to me is to let the light of Christ shine through our work. What an awesome and eternal opportunity.

Contact the Authors For Speaking Inquires:

Tony Johnson:

Insta: @assemblyo15

Twitter: @kickslide

Anthony Di Giovanni (Johnson):

Insta: @antony_digio

Twitter @digiovanniT

Made in the USA
Monee, IL
21 May 2020

31641201R00072